THE DEVIL, DEMONS, AND ANGELS

A Study by Jeff Archer

ONESTONE
BIBLICAL RESOURCES

Published by:
One Stone Press
979 Lovers Lane
Bowling Green, KY 42103

Printed in the United States of America

ISBN 10: 1-941422-02-0
ISBN 13: 978-1-941422-02-1

Supplemental Materials Available:

➢ Answer Key

➢ Downloadable PDF

www.onestone.com

ONE STONE

BIBLICAL RESOURCES

CONTENTS

CONTENTS

WHY STUDY THIS?

The Physical And Spiritual Realms

Two realms exist—the physical and the spiritual. The physical/ material realm consists of the universe with stars, planets, and a vast expanse. On the earth, a variety of life forms exists among the plants and animals. In the spiritual realm, God exists with both good and evil spiritual beings. These beings are called angels, the Devil and his angels called demons.

Man is uniquely physical (made from the dust of the ground) and spiritual (in the image of God) at the same time. From conception, man in his flesh, exists in the physical realm for a limited period of time and interacts with the physical creation. From conception, he also, in his spirit, exists in the spiritual realm for eternity and interacts with God and the spiritual creation. In many ways, man finds it easier to interact with the physical realm. However, man must not only acknowledge and understand the spiritual realm but be led by the spirit and not the flesh.

This lesson discusses the answers to the question of why one should study the subject of the Devil, demons and angels.

The Spiritual Battle
Between Righteousness And Wickedness

1. The book of Revelation gives us a glimpse into events in the spiritual realm taking place simultaneously with events in the physical realm. For example, how did John describe the birth of Jesus (Rev. 12:1-9)? _____
_____
_____

   A. What does this teach us about the desires of Satan? _____
   _____
   _____

2. In the parable of the tares, Jesus told of His work and the work of the Devil. What did the Devil do and why (Matt. 13:24-30, 36-43)? _____
_____
_____

Put on the whole **armor of God**, that you may be able to **stand against** the wiles of the devil. For we do not **wrestle against** flesh and blood, but against principalities, against powers, against the rulers of the **darkness** of this age, against spiritual hosts of wickedness in the **heavenly places**.
--Ephesians 6:11-12

3. How was Jesus' coming to the world described (John 1:5)? _____
_____
_____

This Battle Involves Us

4. Where is the Devil and what is he doing (I Peter 5:8)? ____
_____
_____

5. Where is the struggle of the Christian (Eph. 6:11-12)? ____
_____
_____

We Are Either Children Of God Or Of the Devil

6. Who was the "father" of the Jews with whom Jesus spoke (John 8:44)? _____
_____

   A. Why? _____
_____

7. How does one know whose child he is (1 John 3:8-10)?
_____
_____

The Final Destiny Of The Devil, Demons And Angels

8. Where will the Devil and his angels be cast (Matt. 25:41; Rev. 20:10)? _____
_____

   A. Who will join them (Matt. 25:41)? _____
_____

9. Where were the angels of God in the time of John (Rev. 5:11-12)? _____
_____

10. As John looked into the future, where did he see the angels (Rev. 7:9-12)? _____
_____

11. An abundance of teaching about demons and angels comes from the secular and religious world. If one teaches anything, what should be hsi source (1 Pet. 4:11)?
_____
_____
_____

ORIGINS: THE CREATION BY GOD

1. Who created all things (Col. 1:15-18)? _____
_____

2. What has He created (Col. 1:16)? _____
_____
_____

3. Psalms 148 gives praise to the Lord for all He created. What/who is included within the list (Psa. 148:2)? _____
_____

4. Who were witnesses of the creation of the earth (Job 38:4-7)? _____
_____

5. Thought question. Does any person know when the Devil, demons and angels were created? Was it at the same time as the universe was created? _____
_____
_____

6. In what position was man created in comparison to the angels (Psa. 8:4-5 quoted in Heb. 2:6-8)? _____
_____

   A. Is man to worship angels (Rev. 19:10; 22:8-9)? _____

7. Into what position was man created in comparison to the physical creation (Psa. 8:5-8)? _____
_____

8. What responsibility was given to angels (Jude 6)? _____
_____
_____

9. What are some examples of the teaching from the world concerning the origin of the Devil, demons and/or angels? _____

_____

_____

A. Some say Lucifer refers to the Devil in Isaiah 14:12. To whom does Isaiah say Lucifer refers (Isa. 14:4)? _____

_____

_____

Did God Create The Devil And His Angels Evil?

10. How did Jesus describe the Devil at the beginning (Jn. 8:44)? _____

_____

11. What was the Devil's problem according to Paul (1 Tim. 3:6)? _____

_____

A. Can one know when the Devil became evil? _____

_____

_____

12. What happened to cause some angels to change their relationship with God (2 Peter 2:4, Jude 6)? _____

_____

_____

What is **man** that **You** are **mindful** of him,

And the son of man that You **visit** him?

For You have made him a little **lower** than the **angels,** And You have **crowned him** with glory and honor.

--Psalm 8:4-5

SATAN'S CHARACTER

"In The Beginning"

The Bible offers little introduction to Satan. The Bible record introduces him in the form of a serpent in the garden of Eden (Gen. 3). His conversation with Eve seems to be evidence of a much older and deeper conflict he had with God.

1. How was Satan described in Genesis 3:1? _____
_____
_____

   A. How can one know who this serpent was (Rev. 12:9)? _____
_____

2. What can one learn about Satan's relationship with God from his interaction with Eve (Gen. 3:1-5)? _____
_____

3. In addition to what the serpent told Eve, what else contributed to her sin (Gen. 3:6)?
_____
_____

4. How did God curse the serpent for his role in the sin of Adam and Eve (Gen. 3:14-15)?
_____
_____

5. What does one learn about the Devil from Jesus (John 8:44)? _____
_____
_____

6. What does one learn about the Devil from John (1 John 3:8)? _____
_____
_____

7. What does one learn about the connection between those who sin and the Devil (1 John 3:11-12)? _____
_____
_____
_____

Satan Was "Cast Out" Of Heaven More Than Once

In which you once walked according to the **course** of this **world**, according to the **prince** of the **power** of the air, the **spirit** who now **works** in the sons of **disobedience**.
--Ephesians 2:2

8. When was the Devil cast out of heaven and why (Luke 10:18)? _____
_____
_____

9. When was the Devil cast out of heaven and why (Rev. 12:7-9)? _____
_____
_____

10. Into what place was the Devil cast (Rev. 20:1-3)? _____
_____
_____

11. Into what place will the Devil be cast (Rev. 20:10)? _____
_____
_____

SATAN'S CHARACTER (CONTINUED)

Names/Descriptions Of The Devil

1. The word "Satan" is used 36 times in the New Testament and means "one who lies in wait," "adversary."

   A. What was Satan doing on the earth (Job 1:6-12)? _____
   _____

   B. What warning did Paul give the Christians in Corinth (2 Cor. 2:10-11)? _____
   _____

2. The term "Devil" is used 37 times in the New Testament and means "slanderer" or "accuser." Note, the KJV translates another Greek word that refers to "demons" as "devils". This can be confusing. There is only one Devil.

   A. How persistent is the Devil in his accusing (Rev. 12:10)? _____
   _____

   B. How can the Devil "devour" us (1 Pet. 5:8)? _____
   _____

3. "The tempter."

   A. How is this a fitting name/description of the Devil (Matt. 4:3; 1 Thess. 3:5)? _____
   _____
   _____

4. "Prince of the power of the air."

   A. How is this a fitting name/description of the Devil (Eph. 2:2)? _____
   _____

5. "The god of this age."

    A. How is this a fitting name/description of the Devil (2 Cor. 4:3-4)? _____

    _____

6. "The ruler of this world."

    A. How is this a fitting name/description of the Devil (Jn. 12:31, 14:30, 16:11)? _____

    _____

Devices Of The Devil

7. Paul said he was "not ignorant of his (Satan's) devices" in 2 Cor. 2:11. What does this word "devices" mean? _____

_____

8. Paul talked about the "snare of the devil" (2 Tim. 2:26, 1 Tim. 6:9). What does "snare" mean? _____

_____

_____

9. What did Satan ask to do to Peter (Luke 22:31-32)? _____

_____

_____

    A. How did Satan accomplish this (Luke 22:54-62)? _____

    _____

    _____

10. What did the Devil do to Judas (John 13:2, 21-27)? _____

_____

> Be sober, be vigilant, because your **adversary** the **devil** walks about like a **roaring lion**, seeking whom he may **devour**.
> --1 Peter 5:8

The Devil	
Satan = Adversary	Devil = Accuser
Tempter	prince of the power of the air
god of this age	ruler of this world

Jesus	
Jesus = Savior	Advocate
Mediator	Head of His body, the church
Alpha and Omega	King of Kings

SATAN'S SNARES

Deception

Perhaps the most often used tactic of the Devil is deception. In fact, almost all of his tactics include some element of deception.

1. What lies did the Devil tell Eve (Gen. 3:1-6)? _____
_____
_____

2. How might one be deceived like Eve (2 Cor. 11:2-3)? _____
_____
_____

3. What is Satan able to do (2 Cor. 11:14)? _____
_____
_____

   A. Who else is able to be deceptive (2 Cor. 11:13-15)? _____
_____
_____
_____

   B. Give some modern-day examples of lies of the Devil or "his ministers"? _____
_____
_____

   C. Are his ministers aware they are "his" ministers? _____
_____
_____

4. The New Testament warns us, "Do not be deceived." Please study the following specific warnings and give one modern day lie (attempt by the Devil) to deceive us.

A. 1 Cor. 15:33 - _____
_____

B. Gal. 6:7 - _____
_____

C. Eph. 5:6 - _____

D. James 1:16 - _____

E. 1 Cor. 6:9-10 - _____

And no wonder! For **Satan** himself **transforms** himself into an **angel** of **light**.

--2 Corinthians 11:14

5. In what specific area does Satan try to ensnare us (1 Tim. 6:9)? _____
_____
_____

6. In what specific area does Satan try to ensnare us (2 Tim. 2:24-26)? _____
_____
_____

7. What is the "deceitfulness of sin" (Heb. 3:12-13)? _____
_____
_____
_____

8. What is Satan able to do to deceive (2 Thess. 2:9-10)? __
_____
_____
_____

9. Is it possible to identify and overcome all the lies of the Devil (1 Cor. 10:13)? _____
_____
_____
_____

DEMONS & UNCLEAN SPIRITS

"My initial investigation of Demonology proved to be rather expensive, laborious and frustrating. I bought an armload of current books on Demonology and the Occult only to find that they are, in the main, rather useless. They, generally speaking, are not Biblical. They simply serve as outlets for highly opinionated authors who see an opportunity to cash in on a gullible generation. . . In the main I found that uninspired writings on Demonology largely depend upon personal experiences and personal testimonies. . . . The only safe conclusions to be reached in regard to Demonology, are those based on scripture." Raymond Harris' class material on Demonology, preface.

Old Testament

The term English term "demons" is found 3 times in the Old Testament. Please note that the KJV translates this same term "devils" which causes confusion. There are many demons but only one Devil.

1. To whom were the Israelites NOT to sacrifice (Lev. 17:7)? _____
_____

2. When the children of Israel offered sacrifices to false gods, to whom did God say they offered their sacrifices (Deut. 32:17; Psa. 106:37-38) _____

   A. Do you think the people realized they were sacrificing to demons? _____

New Testament

The term "demon" and "demons" are found 75 times in the New Testament. "Unclean spirits" is also used 10 times and is used interchangeably with "demons".

3. Paul warned against idolatry. To whom did he say one would sacrifice if he sacrificed to idols (1 Cor. 10:20-21)? _____
_____

4. Do demons know who Jesus is (James 2:19)? _____
_____

5. Spirit-beings who serve the Devil are also called (Matt. 25:41)? _____
_____

New Testament Demon Possession

There is no record of demon possession in the Old Testament. The only recorded occurrences took place during the ministry of Christ and twice in the book of Acts.

6. Who had power to cast out demons?

    A. Luke 4:36 _____

    B. Luke 9:1 _____

    C. Luke 10:1,17-20 _____

    D. Acts 5:12-16 _____

    E. Acts 8:5-7 _____

7. Did the disciples ever have problems casting out a demon? Why (Matt. 17:14-21)?
_____
_____

    A. What was the solution? _____

8. Who did Jesus heal? Matt. 12:22 _____

    A. By what power did the Pharisees say He cast out the demon (Matt. 12:24)? Who was that? _____
_____

    B. Why was that accusation not logical? Matt. 12:25-27 _____
_____

    C. By Whose power did Jesus cast out the demon? Matt. 12:28 _____
_____

    D. Whose "house" did Jesus plunder? Matt. 12:29 _____
_____

    E. In what way was the accusation of the Pharisees blasphemy against the Holy Spirit? Matt. 12:31 _____
_____

What are "demons" and "unclean spirits"? 6 possibilities
    1. Spirits of the evil from a pre-Adamic creation
    2. Spirits of a mixed angel-human race – Gen. 6
    3. Spirits of the evil who perished in the flood
    4. Spirits of evil men who have died outside of salvation
    5. The same as fallen angels
    6. (Best Option, JA) Part of the Devil's evil forces whether his "angels" or other evil spirits. "Unclean" in a moral sense.

DEMON POSSESSION

What can be known about "demons" and "unclean spirits"?

1. They are intelligent, able to see into spirit/physical world. They know who Jesus is.

2. They are set for punishment (they knew they would be thrown into the abyss).

3. They have less power than God but more than a man. They could only be cast out by the miraculous power of God.

4. They could affect a man's physical condition but could not force a possessed person into immoral actions.

Occurrences

1. Please read Luke 4:31-37.

A. What did the demons say about who Jesus was? _____
_____

B. What power did the demon(s) have over the man? _____
_____

C. What was the reaction of the people to this miracle? _____
_____

2. Please read Luke 4:40-42.

A. Was being physically sick and having a demon the same thing? _____
_____

B. What did the demons say about who Jesus was? _____
_____

C. What was the reaction of the people to this miracle? __
_____
_____

3. Please read Luke 8:26-40.

A. What did the demons say about who Jesus was? _____
_____
_____

B. What power did the demons have over the man? _____
_____
_____

C. To what place did the demons not want to be cast? __
_____

D. What was the reaction of the people to this miracle? __
_____
_____

E. What did Jesus tell the man from whom the demon was cast to do? _____
_____
_____

4. Please read Matt. 4:24; 8:16-17.

A. What was the reaction of the people to these miracles?
_____
_____

B. What prophecy was fulfilled by Jesus' miracles (Matt. 8:17)? _____
_____
_____
_____

5. Who tried to cast out an evil spirit in the name of Jesus (Acts 19:11-14)? _____
_____
_____

Then they were all amazed and spoke among themselves, saying, "What a **word** this is! For with **authority** and power He **commands** the unclean spirits, and they **come out**."

--Luke 4:36

A. Why would they do this? _____

_____

B. What reaction did the evil spirit have (Acts 19:15-17)? _____

_____

_____

C. What was the reaction of the people who heard (Acts 19:17)? _____

_____

_____

_____

Demon Possession Today

6. Why was demon possession allowed by God? _____

_____

7. Is there any Biblical evidence that demon possession occurs beyond the age of miracles? _____

_____

8. When people teach a person can be possessed by demons today,...

A. What power do they believe the demon has? _____

_____

B. How do they believe a demon is cast out? _____

_____

Pentecostal emphasis—Our sins are caused by outside forces: demons. These demons take control/override our moral decision making power. They must be cast out by the miraculous power of the Holy Ghost.

Calvinist emphasis—Our sins are caused by inside forces: sinful nature inherited from Adam. This sinful nature takes control/overrides our moral decision making power. It must be changed by God's grace.

Truth emphasis—The Devil and his forces seek to influence us from the outside and our fleshly desires from the inside. One's spirit has a sense of ought and can be educated by the word of God. Each one has the power and responsibility to decide. Each one must be forgiven by the blood of Christ for choosing to sin.

A. Why would they do this?

B. What reaction did the evil spirit have (Acts 19:15-17)?

C. What was the reaction of the people who heard (Acts 19:17)?

Demon Possession Today

OUR FIGHT WITH SATAN & HIS ANGELS

The Spiritual Battle Is Real!

1. How powerful is the Devil (1 Peter 5:8)? _____
_____

   A. Can he be resisted? How (1 Peter 5:9)? _____
_____

2. How powerful are temptations (Rom. 3:23)? _____
_____

   A. Can one say "no" to temptation? How (1 Cor. 10:13)? _____
_____
_____

3. Does God tempt us with evil (James 1:13)? _____

   A. Who is responsible for temptations (James 1:14-15)? _____
_____

   B. What does it mean to be "enticed" and from whom does the enticement come?
_____
_____
_____

4. Where is the battle of the Christian fought (Eph. 6:12)? _____
_____

   A. Can Satan and his angels be defeated? How (Eph. 6:10-20)? _____
_____
_____

The Devil Has Been And Will Be Defeated!

5. What curse was pronounced upon Satan (Gen 3:15)? __
_____
_____

6. How did Jesus crush the power of Satan (Heb. 2:9)? ____
_____
_____

> But we see **Jesus**, who was made a little **lower** than the **angels**, for the suffering of **death** **crowned** with **glory** and **honor**, that He, by the grace of God, might taste death **for** **everyone**.
> --Hebrews 2:9

7. Because of the death of Christ, what can one do (Heb. 2:10)? _____
_____

8. In addition to the spiritual death, what other victory does Jesus give us over Satan (Heb. 2:14-15)? _____
_____
_____
_____
_____

A. If one still dies physically, when will our victory come (1 Cor. 15:24-28)? _____
_____
_____

B. What kind of body will one have at the resurrection (1 Cor. 15:51-57)? _____
_____
_____

9. What will be the ultimate end of Satan (Rev. 20:10)? ____
_____
_____

10. What will be the ultimate end of angels who sinned (Jude 6, 2 Peter 2:4)? _____
_____

ANGELS IN THE OLD TESTAMENT

Angels

The word "angel" and "angels" is found 114 times in the Old Testament (largest number in Judges with 22 and Zechariah with 21) and 195 times in the New Testament (largest number in Matthew with 21 and Revelation with 79).

Hebrew - *malak* from the root "to despatch as a deputy; a messenger;" (Strong's) Greek - *aggelos* "a messenger, envoy, one who is sent, an angel, a messenger from God" (Thayer's)

These words normally referred to a spirit-being living in the spiritual realm who was sent as God's messenger to man. A few times the term referred to men who were messengers (Luke 7:24, 27; 9:52; James 2:25) and, specifically, in reference to John the baptizer (Matt. 11:10; Mark 1:2; Luke 7:27).

Position And Nature

1. What position do angels hold in relationship to Jesus (Heb. 1:6-9)? _____

_____

2. Where are angels in relationship to man (Heb. 2:6-8)? _____

_____

3. Are angels physical or spiritual beings (Luke 2:13-15; Gen. 19:1ff)? _____

_____

4. Do the angels have individual personalities (Luke 1:26)? _____

_____

5. Is there any rank among angels (1 Thess. 4:16; Jude 9)? _____

_____

6. Are angels married? Why or why not (Matt. 22:30)? __
   _____
   _____
   _____
   _____

7. Other spirit-beings are also mentioned in the Bible. These are not called "angels". What are they called (Gen. 3:24; Isa. 6:2; Rev. 4:6)? _____
   _____
   _____

Role - Messengers Of God

8. Delivered the message of God - What role did the two angels play in the destruction of Sodom and Gomorrah (Gen. 19:1-22)? _____
   _____
   _____

9. Carried out God's judgment - What role did angels play in the plagues of Egypt (Psa. 78:43-51)? _____
   _____
   _____
   _____

10. Protected, guided God's people - What role did the angel play in the deliverance of Israel (Ex. 14:19-20; 23:20-23)? _____
    _____
    _____

11. "Ordained" the Law of Moses - What role did the angels play in the giving of the Law (Gal. 3:19; Acts 7:38,53)? __
    _____
    _____
    _____
    _____

But we see **Jesus**, who was made a little **lower** than the **angels**, for the suffering of **death** **crowned** with **glory** and **honor**, that He, by the grace of God, might taste death **for** **everyone**. --Hebrews 2:9

ANGELS IN THE OLD TESTAMENT (2)

Role - Messengers Of God (cont.)

Angels = Messengers
1. Delivered the message of God.
2. Carried out God's judgment.
3. Protected, guided God's people.
4. "Ordained" the Law of Moses.

1. What role did the angel play with Israel in Judges 2:1-4? _____
_____

2. What role did an angel play with Israel in 1 Chronicles 21:13-18? _____
_____

3. Although not called angels, spiritual beings had a part in a battle between Elisha
   and the Syrians. What was the servant of Elisha able to see (2 Kings 6:13-17)? _____
_____
_____

4. What role did an angel play in the defeat of the Assyrians (2 Kings 19:35)? _____
_____

5. Who delivered the message of God to Zechariah (Zech. 1:9,11,12,13,14,19: 2:3 etc.)?
_____
_____

"The Angel Of The Lord"

The designation "the Angel of the Lord" occurs 57 times in the Old Testament. (Please
note that the "A" in "Angel" is capitalized by the Bible translators. Capitalizing the "A"
is their interpretation. It is not part of the original manuscript.)

Some believe this "Angel" referred to Jesus coming to earth in the form of a man because the Angel spoke as the LORD. Others believe that "the Angel" is one of the host of angels who, like the prophets, spoke as the LORD.

Please examine the following selected passages and draw your own conclusion.

6. What happened with the Angel of the LORD and Hagar (Gen. 16:7-13)? _____

_____

7. With whom did Jacob wrestle (Gen. 32:24-30)? _____

_____

_____

> But when He again brings the firstborn into the world, He says: "Let **all** the **angels** of God **worship** Him."
>
> --Hebrews 1:6

A. With whom did Jacob wrestle (Hosea 12:3-4)? _____

_____

8. Who spoke with Moses in the burning bush (Ex. 3:2-6)?

_____

_____

9. With whom did Gideon speak (Judges 6:11-24)? _____

_____

_____

10. With whom did Joseph speak (Matt. 1:20-24)? _____

_____

_____

11. In what position is Jesus in comparison to the angels (Heb. 1:5-9)? _____

_____

ANGELS IN THE LIFE OF CHRIST

Role - Messengers Of God (cont.)

Angels = Messengers
   1. Delivered the message of God.
   2. Carried out God's judgment.
   3. Protected, guided God's people.
   4. "Ordained" the Law of Moses.

1. Who spoke with Zacharias about the birth of John (Luke 1:11-18)? _____
_____

   A. Who was this angel and what power did he have (Luke 1:19-25)? _____
   _____

2. Who spoke with Joseph about the birth of Christ (Matt. 1:20-25)? _____
_____

3. Who spoke with Mary about the birth of Jesus (Luke 1:26-38)? _____
_____

4. What message did an angel deliver to the shepherds (Luke 2:8-15)? _____
_____

5. Why did Joseph take his family to Egypt and why did he leave Egypt when he did
(Matt. 2:13,19ff)? _____
_____
_____

6. What did angels do for Jesus (Matt. 4:11; Luke 22:43)? _____
_____

7. Who did Jesus say Nathanael would see "ascending and descending on the Son of
Man" (John 1:51—compare with Gen. 28:12)? _____
_____

> And He said to him, "Most assuredly, I say to you, hereafter you shall see heaven open, and the **angels** of God **ascending** and **descending** upon the **Son of Man**."
>
> --John 1:51

A. What did this mean? _____

_____

_____

8. How many angels were at Jesus' disposal (Matt. 26:53)?

_____

_____

A. Why did they not come and rescue Jesus? _____

_____

_____

9. Who were at the grave of Jesus? What was their purpose (Matt. 28:1-8; Mark 16:5-8; Luke 24:2-8,23; John 20:11-13)? _____

_____

_____

_____

10. What role will the angels play on the Judgment Day?

A. Matt. 13:37-43 _____

_____

_____

_____

B. Matt. 24:36 _____

_____

_____

_____

C. Matt. 25:31-33 _____

_____

_____

_____

D. 2 Thess. 1:6-8 _____

_____

_____

_____

E. 1 Cor. 6:3 _____

_____

_____

_____

ANGELS IN THE NEW TESTAMENT

Role - Messengers Of God (cont.)

Angels = Messengers
  1. Delivered the message of God.
  2. Carried out God's judgment.
  3. Protected, guided God's people.
  4. "Ordained" the Law of Moses.

1. What did an angel do for the apostles in Acts 5:17-20? _____
_____

2. What did an angel do for Peter in Acts 12:7-11? _____
_____

  A. How did Herod die (Acts 12:23)? _____
  _____

3. What did an angel tell Philip to do in Acts 8:26? _____
_____

4. How were Peter and Cornelius brought together (Acts 10:3-22)? _____
_____

5. How did an angel help Paul in Acts 27:23-25? _____
_____

6. Who delivered the message of Jesus to John (Rev. 1:1; 5:2; 7:2; 8:3 etc.)? _____
_____

  A. Who are the angels of the churches (Rev. 2:1,8,12,18;3:1,7,14)? _____
  _____

B. What power/authority did angels have (Rev. 14:17-19; 16:2-17; 20:1)? _____
_____
_____
_____

Role - Messengers Of God (Today)

It is obvious God used angels in the spreading of the gospel in the first century. They did not do any actual teaching of the lost, but they were active in helping the Christians and guiding them to those who needed to hear. Since the age of direct communication has ceased (the revelation has been completed 1 Cor. 13:10; 2 Pet. 1:3; Jude 3), one does not receive direct messages from God through angels today. However, there are indications angels are still interacting with the physical world on our behalf.

7. What indications are there that angels were interested observers in what was happening on the earth? This may imply that they continue to be interested observers today as well.

A. 1 Pet. 1:10-12 _____
_____
_____
_____

B. Eph. 3:10 _____
_____
_____
_____

C. 1 Tim. 3:16 _____
_____
_____
_____

D. 1 Cor. 4:9 _____
_____
_____
_____

"For there **stood by** me this night an **angel** of the God to whom I belong and whom I serve, saying, '**Do not be afraid**...'"

--Acts 27:23-24

ANGELS IN THE NEW TESTAMENT (2)

Role - Messengers Of God (cont.)

Angels = Messengers
1. Delivered the message of God.
2. Carried out God's judgment.
3. Protected, guided God's people.
4. "Ordained" the Law of Moses.

1. Who rejoices when a sinner repents (Luke 15:7,10)? _____
_____

2. When one dies, what role do angels fulfill (Luke 16:22)? _____
_____

3. For whom are angels ministering (Heb. 1:14)? _____
_____

A. Is this an ongoing work which extends to today? _____
_____

4. Who was battling in the spiritual world (Rev.12:7)? _____
_____

   A. Do these spiritual battles continue today? _____
_____

5. What forces, beyond what one can see here on the earth, are battling in the spiritual realm (Eph. 6:10)? _____
_____

6. Who might one entertain (Heb. 13:2)? _____

_____

_____

A. If one entertained an angel, would they know it? _____

_____

_____

7. What was a reason for women to wear the head covering in Corinth (1 Cor. 11:10)? _____

_____

_____

_____

8. Some believe each person has guardian angel. Matthew 18:10 is used to support this view. Please examine this passage and discuss what you think. _____

_____

_____

_____

9. Do some research into some of the modern teachings/ speculations about angels and determine which are supported by Scripture. _____

_____

_____

_____

_____

"Take heed that you do not despise one of these little ones, for I say to you that in heaven **their angels** always **see** the face of **My Father** who is in **heaven**."
--Matthew 18:10